1001

ONE-LINERS

AND SHORT JOKES

1001

ONE-LINERS

AND SHORT JOKES

THE ULTIMATE COLLECTION OF THE FUNNIEST, LAUGH-OUT-LOUD RIB-TICKLERS

GRAHAM CANN

"Laughter is the sun that drives winter from the human face"

VICTOR HUGO

CONTENTS

THE CURTAIN-RAISER

'1001 One-Liners and Short Jokes' is a compilation of some of the most hilarious one-liners that have been told in theatres, clubs, TV and radio over the years. They are short, to the point and loved by people of all ages. It is also a celebration of those wonderfully gifted comedians who have perfected their craft and poured out their talent for our benefit. The likes of Ken Dodd, George Burns and Tommy Cooper have graced the stage and left audiences howling with laughter and demanding more. Who can forget those immortal lines, "I got this dog for my wife. I wish I could make a swap like that every day"?

Indeed, in this world that we are living in today, their craft is needed more than ever. Sadly most of the old music hall greats are no longer with us but a new generation of comics like Tim Vine have taken to the boards and are wowing audiences today in the same one-liner tradition as those in the past. Long may they continue to keep us entertained and to preserve our sanity!

The jokes on the following pages have been gleaned from numerous sources over a number of years and most of them could be told to your local vicar without too much hesitation. I have arranged them in over forty categories for easy reference where you will be able to dip in and find a joke on most topics.

All that is left for me to say is that I hope you enjoy this book as much as I did compiling it.

ADDICTIONS

People say I've got no willpower but I've quit smoking loads of times.

I rolled up a stiff carpet and smoked it. I'm on hard rugs.

I just bought some weed called 'The Koran'. It comes with a warning: 'Burning this shit really can get you stoned'.

If smoking's so bad for you, how come it can cure dead salmon?

It's hard to explain puns to kleptomaniacs because they always take things literally.

It's OK to smoke weed in the rain but don't in hail.

Graham Cann

I bought a pair of shoes off a drug dealer. I don't know what he laced them with but I've been tripping all day.

A mate of mine admitted to being addicted to brake fluid. When I quizzed him, he said he could stop at any time.

I took a urine test at the hospital yesterday. This kleptomania's getting out of hand.

I backed a horse last week at ten to one. It came in at a quarter past four.

It's easy to become addicted to helter-skelters. It's a downward spiral.

I used to be addicted to soap but I'm clean now.

I couldn't hold a candle to my grandfather. He was an alcoholic.

Gambling addiction hotlines might get a lot more gamblers if every tenth caller was a winner.

I have kleptomania. When it gets bad, I take something for it.

I used to be addicted to the hokey cokey but I turned myself around.

'Dad, are we pyromaniacs?' 'We arson'.

I used to be addicted to swimming but I'm proud to say I've been dry for six years.

My dad has a weird hobby. He collects bottles. Sounds so much better than alcoholic.

Apparently, smoking cannabis can affect your short-term memory. Well, if that's true, what do you think smoking cannabis does?

Graham Cann

ARTS AND CRAFTS

At hospital over the weekend, I heard a load of patients reciting Scottish poetry. Apparently it was a serious Burns unit.

I've been reading a book about anti-gravity. It's impossible to put down.

I recently got crushed by a pile of books but I suppose I've only got my shelf to blame.

My room-mate has just lost one of my Mr Men books. No more 'Mr Nice Guy'.

Bilbo Baggins of the Shire died in bed last night after an overdose of Viagra. I guess old Hobbits die hard.

I'm studying anthropology. I went to my local library and said 'Do you keep books on pygmies?' The girl said 'No, only on shelves'.

I've just read a book on the psychology of camping. It was in tents.

I'm reading a book about the internal workings of F15 fighter bombers. It went right over my head.

Today's a good day for going into a bookstore and asking where the self-help section is.

A bit of advice: Never read a pop-up book on giraffes.

I do portraits of boxers. I can knock them out really quickly.

Someone left some plasticine at my home yesterday. I don't know what to make of it.

I'm currently reading a book called 'My Life' by Bill Clinton. It freaked me out. I didn't think he knew anything about me.

I have a book in my toilet all about the Velvet Underground. There's nothing like a Lou Reed.

I'm reading a book called 'The History of Glue'. I couldn't put it down.

I like to go to bookstores and say to the shop assistant "I'm looking for a book called 'How To Deal With Rejection Without Killing'. Have you got it?"

They told me I'd never be any good at poetry because I'm dyslexic. But so far I've made three jugs and a vase and they're lovely.

A woman walked into a library and asked for a book on euphemisms. So the librarian took her up the rear aisle and let her have it.

My grandad always said that you could never judge a book by its cover. And it was for that reason he lost his job as chair of the British Book Cover Awards panel.

I'm reading a horror story in Braille. Something bad is about to happen........I can feel it.

CHILDREN

Our local school has become an Academy. It's sponsored my IKEA. Standards may be fine but assembly takes ages.

You spend the first two years teaching children to walk and talk. Then you spend the next sixteen years telling them to sit down and shut up.

I think children are like Marmite. You either love them or keep them at the back of the cupboard next to the piccalilli.

As a kid I was made to walk the plank. We couldn't afford a dog.

British scientists have demonstrated that cigarettes can harm your children. Fair enough, use an ashtray.

I was messing about in this lesson and the teacher told me to go outside. I was petrified. It was a flying lesson.

Be nice to your kids. They'll choose your nursing home.

When I was a child we had a sandpit. It was a quicksand pit. I was an only child.....eventually.

When I turned two, I was really anxious because I'd doubled my age in a year. I thought if this keeps up, by the time I'm six I'll be ninety.

When your children are teenagers you should have a dog, so at least someone in the house is happy to see you.

I had a happy childhood. My dad would put me inside a tyre and roll me down the hill. They were Goodyears.

I don't know what to get my nine year old Scouse nephew for his birthday so I put £20 in his nan's purse.

Graham Cann

We named our little girl after her mother.   Passive Aggressive Psycho turns five next week.

I had a tough time at school. The other kids used to push me around and call me lazy. I loved that wheelchair.

CHRISTMAS

The main reason why Santa's so jolly is because he knows where all the bad girls live.

My girlfriend said she'd like an animal skin coat for Christmas. So I bought her a donkey jacket.

Is the fear of getting stuck in a chimney Santaclaustrophobia?

OK I've had it with cold turkey now! I'm getting back on the heroin.

I thought I'd come across a mass grave of snowmen. It turned out to be a field of carrots.

Why is it harder to buy an advent calendar? Because their days are numbered.

How do you know Santa's been in your garden shed? You've got three extra hoes.

Don't forget that today is all about that amazing, kind man who helped strangers, died and was reborn. Happy 'Doctor Who' Day everyone.

I asked my wife what she wanted for Christmas. She told me that nothing would make her happier than a diamond necklace. So I bought her nothing.

Why did no-one bid for Rudolph and Blitzen on eBay? They were two deer.

You never see Santa in hospital because he has private elf care.

What's the difference between snowmen and snowladies? Snowballs.

It's tradition in our family that we always have a Christmas jumper. It's my job to talk them down.

CREATURES

One in four frogs is a leap frog.

I used to live near a farm and every time I passed the cows in the field, I'd shout abuse at them. Turns out I'm dairy intolerant.

What do you get when you cross a kangaroo with a sheep? A woolly jumper.

What do you call a cow with one leg shorter than the other? Lean beef.

I have a horse called Mayo. Mayo neighs.

This bloke ran over a hare so he stopped his car, got out and gave the hare a swig from his hip flask. All of a sudden, the hare jumped up and ran off into the bushes. His friend said 'That's amazing! What have you got in your flask?' He said 'Hare restorer'.

What do you call the soft tissue between a shark's teeth? A slow swimmer.

My budgie broke his leg today so I made him a little splint out of two Swan Vesta matches and his little face lit up as he tried to walk. Unfortunately, I'd forgotten to remove the sandpaper from the bottom of the cage.

Two fish sitting in a tank. One turns to the other and says 'How do you drive this thing?'

How does a bull warm himself on a cold night? He slips into a Jersey.

I don't do jokes about an elephant who's packed his trunk and left the circus. Not on your Nellie.

Graham Cann

Polygamy. The art of parrot folding.

If you choke a Smurf, what colour will it turn?

My daughter's horse will only come out of the stable when it gets dark. It's becoming a nightmare.

Circus lions. They never get a fair crack of the whip.

How do chickens dance? Chick to chick.

I'm keeping maggots warm in my mouth for fishing. Will they do me any harm? I wait with baited breath.

Eagles may soar but weasels don't get sucked into jet engines.

Sponges grow in the oceans. I wonder how much deeper the oceans would be if that didn't happen.

A man walks into a zoo. The only animal in it is a dog. It's a shitzu.

Why do you never see a hippopotamus hiding in a tree? Because they're really good at it.

I can't remember the name of my homing pigeon but I'm sure it'll come back to me.

Hedgehogs. Why can't they just share the hedge?

What do you call a dog with no legs? It doesn't matter – it's not going to come.

So I saw this dolphin serial killer. It was Jack the Flipper.

What do you call a little amphibian who never goes out? Hermit the Frog.

Graham Cann

My dog always misinterprets things I say to him. I say 'Heel' and he goes down the local hospital and does what he can.

There were two worms in the graveyard making love in dead Earnest.

What do you call a big pile of kittens? A Meowntain.

I visited the local RSPCA today. It was so small. You couldn't swing a cat in there.

What weighs two tons and wears a flower behind its ear? A hippy-potamus.

The only reason cows wear bells is because their horns don't work.

The best place to weigh whales is at a whale weigh station.

I've got a gun made out of a dozen pigs. It's a 12-boar.

I've got a chicken proof lawn. It's impeccable.

This chicken came up to me and said 'I can't find my eggs'. I said 'You've probably mislaid them'.

I went to an abattoir yesterday. While I was there, I slipped on a piece of liver and then fell head first into a basin of cow's intestines. It was truly offal.

Why did the chicken commit suicide? To get to the other side.

How come oysters never donate to charity? Because they're shellfish.

30% of car accidents in Sweden involve a moose. I say don't let them drive.

Graham Cann

I saw this mallard eating a burger. It was McDonald Duck.

I said to this bloke 'A bird like a swallow just flew past me.'
He said 'Swift?' I said 'Like the clappers'.

I've just written a book on penguins. On reflection, paper
would have been better.

Why do elephants have big ears? Because Noddy wouldn't
pay the ransom.

A cat hijacked a plane, stuck a pistol into the pilot's face
and demanded: 'Take me to the Canaries!'

The other morning I shot a giant rat in my pyjamas. What
the hell he was doing in my pyjamas I'll never know.

This shepherd said to me, 'I've got 68 sheep. Would you
like to round them up for me?' I said 'OK, you've got 70'.

With all this shite on the TV these days, I think it's about time our parrot went back in its cage.

I'm an avid campaigner for the preservation of endangered species. You should taste my panda jam.

If there's a storm going on outside, our cat scratches everything in sight. When it rains, it paws.

What lies on its back, a hundred feet in the air? A dead centipede.

Two dead canaries on eBay. They're not going cheep.

Who collects frog spawn? Naughty frogs.

Our cat jumped into the washing machine yesterday but at least it died in Comfort.

Graham Cann

Hummingbirds are just regular birds that don't know the words.

What do you call an alligator in a string vest? An investigator.

Whoever coined the phrase 'Quiet as a mouse' has never stepped on one.

My horse doesn't go out much. He's a shire horse.

Why can't you hear a pterodactyl urinate? Because the P is silent.

What do you call a fish with no eyes? Fsh.

My cat is recovering from a massive stroke.

What do you call a deer with no eyes? No eye deer.

My son asked for a pet spider for his birthday so I went to our local pet shop and they wanted £70. I thought 'I can get one cheaper off the web'.

I said to my friend 'I'm thinking of getting a Labrador'. He said 'Have you seen how many of their owners go blind?'

A lorry load of tortoises has crashed into a train load of terrapins. It was turtle disaster.

My dog barks at everyone. Still, what can you expect from a cross-breed?

I saw this extinct bird with a hunchback. It was Quasidodo.

I've never slept with a fish. I'm halibut.

I've got a horse called Treacle. He's got golden stirrups.

I removed the shell from my racing snail to make him go faster but, if anything, it's made him more sluggish.

Black Beauty. Now there's a dark horse.

What's the difference between a kangaroo and a kangaroot? One is an Australian mammal, the other is a Geordie stuck in a lift.

What's the difference between a hippo and a Zippo? One is really heavy, the other is a little lighter.

What's orange and sounds like a parrot? A carrot.

What's got twelve legs, one eye and four tails? Three blind mice and half a kipper.

This bloke told me he pulled off his boxers before going to bed. I said to him 'You spoil those dogs'.

When the elephant stepped on the grape it let out a little whine.

A chicken crossing the road is poultry in motion.

A leopard can never play hide and seek. He's always spotted.

I cooked Pancakes this morning. I was thrilled but my children weren't. Apparently he was their favourite rabbit.

I've got the memory of an elephant. I remember one time I went to a zoo and saw an elephant.

DEATH

I've been asked to take part in a crime scene reconstruction of a murdered campanologist for Crimewatch. Apparently I'm a dead ringer.

Mike tragically drowned last week. At the funeral, we got him a wreath in the shape of a lifebelt. Well, it's what he would have wanted.

Some people say I've got the legs of a dancer. But until they find the rest of the body, the police have got nothing on me.....

My uncle was crushed by a piano. His funeral was very low key.

Will glass coffins be a success? Remains to be seen.

About a month before he died, my uncle had his back covered in lard. After that, he went downhill fast.

My grief counsellor has just died. He was so good, I don't give a shit.

I've just got back from the funeral of my best friend. He died after being hit on the head with a tennis ball. It was a lovely service.

How do you define a will? It's a dead giveaway.

I intend to live forever……or die trying.

What happens when you get scared half to death twice?

A man has died after falling into a vat of coffee. It was instant.

Graham Cann

A Chinese man faked his death but his family were suspicious. They didn't bereave him.

I saw an ad for burial plots. I thought to myself 'That's the last thing I need'.

I met a Dutch girl with inflatable shoes last week and phoned her up to arrange a date. Unfortunately, she'd popped her clogs.

My grandad gave me some sound advice on his deathbed. He said that it's worth shelling out on good speakers.

A friend of mine always wanted to be run over by a steam train. When it happened, he was chuffed to bits.

The man who invented Velcro has died. RIP.

A Mexican stuntman died while making a film. At his funeral, his mother approached the director and said 'Jesus died for your scenes'.

The Grim Reaper came for me last night and I beat him off with a vacuum cleaner. Talk about Dyson with death.

I'm not afraid to die. I just don't want to be there when it happens.

I'll tell you what makes my blood boil. Crematoriums.

I want to die peacefully in my sleep like my grandfather. Not screaming and yelling like the passengers in his car.

Sad news. Yesterday the man who invented predictive text has pissed away. His funfair is next monkey.

Graham Cann

<u>DENTISTS</u>

He never smiles. Not because he's got bad teeth. It's just that his gums don't fit.

I went to my dentist the other day. He said 'I've got some good news and some bad news'. I said 'What's the good news?' He said 'Your teeth are fine'. I said 'So what's the bad news?' He said 'Your gums have got to come out'.

What's the best time to visit your dentist? Tooth-hurtie.

I went to my dentist. He opened my mouth and said 'Say aaahhhh'. I said 'Why?' He said 'My dog's just died'.

A friend of mine won Dentist of the Year. All he got was a little plaque.

I didn't realise my uncle had a false tooth until it came out in conversation.

A local Buddhist monk went to see his dentist but refused all the drugs he was offered. He wanted to transcend dental medication.

Dentistry can be such a depressing job. You're always looking down in the mouth.

This joke is about people with crooked teeth. Brace yourself!

Graham Cann

<u>DOCTORS</u>

'Doctor, I keep getting the urge to purchase a big white bear from the Arctic'.
'You've got buy polar disorder'.

'Doctor, I'm sick and tired of finishing crosswords so quickly'.
'Try not to get two down'.

A man went to see an eye doctor. The receptionist asked him what was wrong. He said 'I keep seeing spots in front of my eyes'. She said 'Have you seen a doctor?' He said 'No, just spots'.

'Doctor, I can't pronounce my F's or my T's'.
'Well, you can't say fairer than that'.

A bloke goes to his doctor with hearing problems. His doctor said 'Can you describe the symptoms?' He said 'Yes. Homer's a fat, yellow, lazy bastard and Marge is a skinny bird with big blue hair'.

'Doctor, the whole world's ganging up on me'.
'Hold on a minute. Hey lads, he's in here!'

'Doctor, I think I'm addicted to Twitter'.
'I'm sorry, I don't follow you'.

My doctor said I'd be lucky to reach 50. That's the last time I give him a lift in my Robin Reliant.

'Doctor, I think I'm a cat'.
'How long's this been going on?'
'Since I was a kitten'.

This bloke went to his doctor with a piece of lettuce sticking out of his arse. 'Ah yes' said his doctor 'that's just the tip of the Iceberg'.

A guy goes into a psychiatrist's office wearing only cling film shorts. The shrink said 'I can clearly see you're nuts'.

'Doctor, I've hurt my arm in several places'.
'Well don't go there anymore'.

A man came round in hospital after a serious accident. He shouted 'I can't feel my legs!' The doctor said 'I know you can't. I had to amputate your arms'.

'Doctor, people keep taking the mickey out of me because I keep thinking I'm a cricket ball'.
'Howzat?'
'Don't you start!'

'Doctor, I can't stop singing The Green Green Grass of Home'.
'That sounds like Tom Jones syndrome'.
'Is that common?'
'It's not unusual'.

How do you confuse a Scottish doctor? Tell him you have 'knee problems'.

'Doctor, I keep thinking people are ignoring me'.
'Next!'

'Doctor, I think I'm a pair of curtains'.
'Pull yourself together'.

'Doctor, I think I'm a road bridge'.
'What's come over you?'
'A lorry, two cars and a motor bike'.

Graham Cann

A man goes to his doctor with a strawberry growing out of his head. So he gave him some cream to put on it'.

I went to the doctors and he said 'Go to Bournemouth, it's great for the flu'. So I went and I got it.

I went to the doctor and he mentioned antiseptic. I said I've got nothing against the Jews.

'Doctor, I keep thinking I'm a German vodka'.
'Schnapps out of it'.

My doctor told me I was turning into an airport. I said 'Is it terminal?'

I went to my GP and told him I'd been hit over the head with a pair of bongos. He said I had slight percussion.

'Doctor, I get heartburn every time I eat birthday cake'.
'Next time, try taking off the candles'.

My doctor told me that jogging could add years to my life. He was right. I feel ten years older already.

'Doctor, could you give me something for my liver?'
'Would half a pound of onions be OK?'

'Doctor, I keep dreaming my eyes change colour'.
'It's just a pigment of your imagination'.

My doctor told me I needed to break into a sweat once a day so I told him I'd start lying to the wife.

I went to the doctor's to ask if he had anything for the wind. So he gave me a kite.

Graham Cann

ENTERTAINMENT

The police raided Bob Geldof's home this morning. They discovered Amphetamines, Smack and Ganja but couldn't find his other daughter.

I'll tell you an actor who's rubbish. Dustbin Hoffman.

Jonathan Ross was arrested in IKEA for stealing a food mixer. He said it was worth the whisk.

When I was working at Burger King's, Andrew Lloyd Webber came in and asked for two Whoppers. I said 'You're good looking and your musicals are great'.

RIP Patrick Moore. No more Mr Night Sky.

Apparently, Marti Pellow has discovered he has arthritis. He feels it in his fingers, he feels it in his toes.....

Chris Eubank has just written a book about ethics. If it's a success, his next one will be about Kent.

One actor is known to berate the Bible and that's Christian Slater.

RIP Vidal Sassoon. He never forgot his roots and he was worth a bob or two.

Katie Price can't mention her love life on Twitter. It involves more than 280 characters.

So I bought this DVD and in the Extras it said 'Deleted Scenes'. When I had a look there was nothing there.

Andrew Lloyd Webber's new musical is about a fizzy drink – 'The Fanta of the Opera'.

TV is called a medium because anything well done is rare.

Graham Cann

I just watched a documentary on the uses of the pick axe. It was ground breaking stuff.

Children shouldn't watch big band performances on TV – too much sax and violins.

The soap Casualty is now in its twenty-sixth year. Ironically, it's not getting any better.

There's a TV documentary about a charity asking for donations in the form of time-keeping devices. I might give it a watch.

My favourite film is Clint Eastwood's classic 'The Unforgiven'. At the moment, they're working on the sequel called 'Look, I Said I'm Sorry'.

I saw this film about prehistoric pigs – 'Jurassic Pork'.

I saw the film 'A Bridge Too Far'. The film before that, the whole cast drowned. It was called 'A Bridge Not Far Enough'.

Darth Vader had a corrupt brother, Taxi Vader.

The lead actor in the local pantomime, Aladdin, was sexually abused on stage last night. To be fair, the audience did try to warn him……….

A new film about Margaret Thatcher has been given an 18 certificate. It's upsetting for miners.

I like to hold hands in the cinema which always seems to startle strangers.

A new sequel to The Exorcist' is being filmed. In this version, a woman hires the devil to get the priest out of her son.

Graham Cann

What do you call Postman Pat when he's retired? Pat.

The evening news is where they begin with 'Good evening' and then proceed to tell you why it isn't.

I was watching the Bermuda Philharmonic Orchestra and half way through, the bloke on the triangle disappeared.

I'm making a TV series about plane hijacking. We just shot the pilot.

I saw a documentary on how ships are put together. Riveting!

Yoko Ono has been signed up for the next series of 'I'm A Celebrity Get Me Out Of Here'. Show bosses think she'll do really well since she's been living off a dead Beatle for over 30 years.

A Spanish magician was doing a magic trick. He said 'Uno, dos.........' and then disappeared without a trace.

There's so much nudity on TV these days. I just sit there shaking my fist.......

This antique dealer came up to me and said 'What do you think of the Chinese dynasty?' I said I thought it was very badly dubbed.

EVERYDAY OBJECTS

What's long and hard and makes women groan?   An ironing board.

I used to file my nails but then I thought 'What's the point of keeping them?'

The other day I sat on a hairdryer.   That put the wind up me.

I've decided to sell my vacuum cleaner.   It was just collecting dust.

I got home and the phone was ringing.   I picked it up and said 'Who's speaking?'   And a voice said 'You are'.

Hey, if anyone knows how to fix broken hinges, my door's always open.

When a clock's hungry, it goes back four seconds.

I bought a new deodorant stick today. The instructions were to remove the wrapper and push up bottom. I can hardly walk since I did it but when I break wind, the room smells really nice.

I just saw a digital radio going cheap because it's stuck on full volume. I can't turn that down!

I've spilt stain remover on my trousers. How do I get that out?

He said 'I'm going to chop off the bottom of one of your trouser legs and put it in a library. I thought 'That's a turn-up for the books'.

Why did the broken clock phone the despotic ruler? Desperate times call for desperate measures.

Graham Cann

I've got a front door made of sponge. Don't knock it!

I've decided to marry a pencil. I can't wait to introduce the parents to my bride 2B.

Whiteboards are remarkable.

When you make quick drying cement, there are no hard and fast rules.

Have you tried that new 007 glue? It Bonds in seconds.

I have a step ladder. I never knew my real ladder.

Man, I love my furniture. Me and my recliner go way back........

Male cribs. They should be boycotted.

I'd like to tell some chimney jokes. I've got a stack of them and the first one's on the house.

Somebody just gave me a shower radio. Thanks a lot! I guess there's no better place to dance than on a slippery surface next to a glass door.

I had a survey done on my house. 8 out of 10 people said they really quite liked it.

FAMILIES

My 13 year old niece is already taking heroin. It's amazing how fast they shoot up these days.

As a family we couldn't decide whether to have our granny cremated or buried so in the end we let her live.

I always go to work wearing baggy trousers in honour of my favourite band. My wife thinks it's Madness.

I asked my mum if I was ugly. She said 'I told you not to call me mum in front of people'.

My wife accused me of being a transvestite. I was mad so I packed her things and left.

A boy was born who had Indian, Chinese, Irish and Italian grandmothers but they couldn't decide on a name for him. Then it hit them – they called him Ravi O'Lee.

My father only hit me once but he used a Volvo.

I surprised my wife with a mink coat. She'd never seen me in one before.

I was raised an only child which really annoyed my sister.

It wasn't until I married that I discovered my wife was really a redhead. No hair, just a red head.

My dad's liver is inside his left knee, his kidneys are on his elbows and his spleen is on the side of his head. Still, his heart's in the right place.

Graham Cann

I told my niece that I saw a moose on the way to work this morning. She said 'How do you know he was on his way to work?'

When my daughter was born she had jaundice. She was small, round and yellow. We called her Melony.

My wife came home from work crying and asking me to console her. So I hit her over the head with my X-Box.

I could tell my parents hated me. My bath toys were a toaster and a radio.

I ordered a chair for my mother-in-law but I had to send it back. The plug was faulty.

My auntie Marge has been ill for so long we changed her name to 'I can't believe she's not better'.

My wife accused me of being immature. I told her to get out of my fort.

Last night I slept like a baby. I woke up three times, wet myself twice and cried myself back to sleep.

My wife and I were married in a public toilet. It was a marriage of convenience.

The mother-in-law phoned today and said 'Come quick, I think I'm dying'. I said 'Phone me back when you're sure'.

I've just been informed that a distant relative has left me a priceless watch in her will. I hope it's not a wind-up.

My wife told me to stop impersonating a flamingo. I had to put my foot down.......

Our family has a genetic predisposition to diarrhoea. It runs in our jeans.

I told my wife she was drawing her eyebrows too high. She looked surprised.

When I was six my family moved to a new city but fortunately I was able to track them down.

One day I saw my dad slumped over his lawnmower crying his eyes out. I said to my mum 'What's the matter with him?' She said 'He's going through a rough patch'.

Our grandmother was a very cultivated lady. She was born in a greenhouse.

Our son was born deaf and blind. It was really hard breaking the news to him.

I'm working on my mother-in-law's grave today. She thinks I'm digging a pond.

Grandad walked into the room with his tackle out smothered in boot polish. He misheard when we told him to turn his clock back.

I haven't spoken to my wife for 18 months. I don't like to interrupt her.

My wife and I were happy for 20 years. Then we met.

By the time a man realises his father was right, he has a son who thinks he's wrong.

My mother never saw the irony in calling me a son-of-a-bitch.

My father told me to invest my money in bonds. So I bought 100 copies of Goldfinger.

Graham Cann

Sad news to share. My plumber has just separated from his wife Florence after 30 years of marriage. He walked into the living room and said 'It's over Flo'.

What's pink and wrinkly and hangs out your trousers? Your mum.

My father was a man of few words. He said to me 'Son………….'

What's worse than ants in your pants? Uncles.

Does my wife think I'm a control freak? I haven't decided yet.

I'm sure wherever my dad is, he's looking down on me. He's not dead, just very condescending.

My wife just found out I replaced our bed with a trampoline. She hit the roof.

My wife cooked me a full breakfast yesterday but forgot the toast. I couldn't help it, I went berserk. It turns out I'm lack toast intolerant.

I accidentally handed my wife a glue stick instead of her lipstick. She still isn't talking to me.

I always take my wife morning tea in my pyjamas. But is she grateful? No! She says she'd rather have it in a cup.

My grandfather was always going on about, in the old days, how people would leave their back doors open. That's probably why his submarine sank.

When I was a kid, my father used to hit me with a camera. I still get flashbacks.

I have mixed race parents. My father prefers the 100 metres. My mother, on the other hand, is Pakistani.

'What's a couple?' I asked my mum. She said '2 or 3'. Which probably explains why her marriage collapsed.

I cleaned the attic with my wife the other day. Now I can't get the cobwebs out of her hair.

FOOD AND DRINK

It all starts innocently, mixing chocolate and Rice Krispies but before you know it, you're adding raisins and marshmallows – it's a rocky road.

I said to the baker 'How come all your cakes are 50p and that one's £1?' He said 'That's Madiera cake'.

I burnt my Hawaiian pizza today. Should have put it on Aloha setting.

I said to the waiter 'Have you got a game pie?' He said 'We certainly have……it's fought its way out of the oven twice'.

I said to the waiter 'How long will my spaghetti be?' He said 'I don't know – we never measure it'.

Graham Cann

Alcohol should be served in Capri Sun pouches. When you can no longer get the straw in the hole, you've had enough.

I couldn't sleep last night so I got up at 3am and made tea in my pyjamas. I couldn't find the teapot anywhere.

Someone threw Chinese soup all over me this morning. It was won-ton violence.

Then there was the sadist chef who enjoyed beating eggs and whipping cream.

Jokes about white sugar are rare. Jokes about brown sugar – demerara.

I went to a restaurant that serves 'breakfast at any time'. So I ordered French toast during the Renaissance.

The best way to make an apple crumble is to torture it for 10 minutes.

One tequila, two tequila, three tequila, floor!

Bakers trade bread recipes on a knead-to-know basis.

Dijon vu – the same mustard as before.

What is the world's most favourite wine? 'I don't like Brussels sprouts'.

I opened my chocolate bar today and inside the wrapper it said 'Loser'. Now that really hurt because there was no competition

'Waiter, this coffee tastes like mud'. 'Well sir, it was ground only 10 minutes ago'.

I've got an eating disorder. I go coffee first, then pudding and then the main course.

Graham Cann

I bought some Armageddon cheese today. It said on the packet 'Best Before End Date'.

What goes in dry, comes out wet and pleases two people? A tea bag.

I just realised that tofu is over-rated. It's just a curd to me.

I know lemons are sharp but try using one to carve a turkey.

A bloke goes into the chippie and says to the bloke behind the counter 'Cod and chips twice'. He said 'I heard you the first time'.

I remember once we had a candlelit dinner. Everything was undercooked.

Most pizza jokes are pretty cheesy.

One armed butlers. They can take it but they can't dish it out.

I went to a restaurant the other day called 'A Taste of the Raj'. The waiter hit me with a stick and got me to build a complicated railway system.

A new EU directive stating that all meat pies should be wrapped in tin has been foiled.

I like to drink my brandy neat but sometimes I take my tie off and leave my shirt out.

Aperitif. French for a set of dentures.

Last night I fell asleep on a bed of rice. I was out as soon as my head hit the pilau.

I used to think an ocean of soda existed but it was just a Fanta sea.

It was a shame about the Italian chef with the terminal illness. He's just pastaway.

I'm on a seafood diet. Every time I see food, I eat it.

What do you get if you divide the circumference of a pumpkin by its diameter?   Pumpkin pi.

Whenever I buy rocket salad, it always goes off before I can eat it.

What is a honeymoon salad? Lettuce alone without any dressing.

I hate all confectionery...........bar humbug.

Every time someone calls me fat I get so depressed I cut myself...................a piece of cake.

1001 One-Liners and Short Jokes

Cadbury's are bringing out a new oriental chocolate bar - a Chinese Wispa.

I really need to confront my fear of German sausages but I fear the wurst.

I went into the kitchen and found my fridge had exploded. I think something may have gone off in there.

I must have eaten too much salmon. I just ran up an escalator that was coming down.

I tried sniffing coke once but the ice cubes got stuck in my nose.

How does Teflon stick to the pan?

Alphabet spaghetti warning: 'May contain N U T S'.

Graham Cann

Apparently there's a new flavour of dog food coming out. It's going to be called 'Postman Pate'.

The potato is like the Katie Price of food. It'll go with pretty much anything.

Our local ice cream man was found dead on the floor of his ice cream van covered in hundreds and thousands. The police say he topped himself.

I said 'Waiter, this lobster's only got one claw'. He said 'He's been in a fight'. I said 'Well give me the winner'.

I'm on a whisky diet. I've lost three days already.

Chopsticks are one of the reasons why the Chinese never invented custard.

I went to a really energetic 'Seafood Disco' last week…….and pulled a mussel.

My friend drowned in a bowl of muesli. He was pulled in by a strong currant.

A man walked into a bar with a roll of tarmac under his arm and said 'A pint please and one for the road'.

A jump lead walked into a bar. The barman said 'I'll serve you but don't start anything'.

A sandwich walked into a bar. The barman said 'Sorry we don't serve food in here'.

I went to an Indian restaurant and I thought 'This smells familiar'. Do you ever get that? Deja vindaloo.

I'd have a coffee but it's not my cup of tea.

Did you know Peter Pan had a brother called Deep?

Graham Cann

Venison's dear, isn't it?

What was the best thing before sliced bread?

So I said to this bloke 'My favourite colour's a bluey green'.
He said 'Azure'. I said 'I'm certain'.

This bloke said to me 'Do you think there's life on Mars?' I
said 'Without a doubt. I can see at least two wasps round
the wrapper'.

What's the difference between roast beef and pea soup?
Anyone can roast beef........

This spaceship landed in front of me and out of it stepped
a 5 metre diameter cream bun. It was one of those extra
cholesterols.

Interesting fact of the day. A steak and kidney pie in
Barbados will cost you £2.50 and a mince and onion pie in

St Lucia will cost you £3.00. Those are the pie rates of the Caribbean.

I just burned 2000 calories. Serves me right for having a nap while the brownies were cooking in the oven.

Onions make me sad. A lot of people don't realise that.

My wife is on a tropical fruit diet so the house is full of fruit. It's enough to make a mango crazy.

I knew I shouldn't have had the seafood. I'm feeling a little eel.

How do the Chinese make a beer recipe? With a brewprint.

What do you give a cannibal who's late for dinner? The cold shoulder.

FRIENDS

The other day I sent my girlfriend a huge pile of snow. I rang her up and said 'Do you get my drift?'

I've got a friend who's a very tall blade of grass. He's easily swayed.

I said to this bloke 'Some friends and I have been talking about you'. He said 'You disgust me'. I said 'We did'.

My girlfriend told me she's leaving me because I keep pretending to be a Transformer. I said 'No, wait! I can change'.

Never laugh at your girlfriend's choices.........you're one of them.

I used to have a girlfriend who was absolutely beautiful – a body like a Greek statue. Completely pale and no arms.

My girlfriend bought a cook book called 'Cheap and Easy Vegetarian Cooking'. Which is perfect for her because not only is she a vegetarian...........

I almost had a psychic girlfriend but she left me before we met.

When I see lovers' names carved in trees, I don't think it's sweet. I just think it's surprising how many people bring a knife on a date.

I told my girlfriend I had a job in a bowling alley. She said 'Tenpin?' I said 'No, it's permanent'.

My girlfriend thinks I'm a stalker. Well, she's not exactly my girlfriend.......yet.

Graham Cann

I have a friend in North Korea. I said 'How's things?' He said 'Can't complain'.

I usually meet my boyfriend at 12:59 because I like that one-to-one time.

A friend of mine tried to annoy me with bird puns but I soon realised toucan play at that game.

My girlfriend ditched me for a fisherman. I was gutted.

I've got a friend who's fallen in love with two school bags. He's bi-satchel.

My friend came from a broken home. His dad was a shocker at DIY.

My mate's girlfriend is mute and communicates by embroidery. It's her vision of sign language, sew to speak.

My boyfriend broke up with me after I stole his wheelchair but he'll come crawling back.

My girlfriend hates it when I make jokes about her weight. She needs to lighten up.

I went to the pub with my girlfriend last night. The locals were shouting 'paedo' at me just because my girlfriend is 21 and I'm 50. It completely spoilt our 10th anniversary.

Graham Cann

<u>GARDENING</u>

I used to get paid £50 an hour just to rake up leaves from other people's gardens. I was raking it in.

I heard a rumour that they were giving away horse manure at my local fair so I went down there to check. It was bullshit.

I spent most of today pruning. I was just chucking prunes at people.

I've heard the Incredible Hulk is a good gardener. He's got green fingers.

I thought I'd pour beer over my garden before planting the lawn. I hoped it would come up half cut.

My wife asked me if I thought we needed new garden furniture. I'm sitting on the fence.

How do you make an apple puff? Chase it round the garden.

I know someone who was arrested and the next day he was in his garden sitting on a haystack. He's been let out on bale.

I don't buy my flowers from monks. I like to do my bit to prevent florist friars.

Yet again someone has added more soil to my allotment. The plot thickens......

I bought some French paving slabs for my garden today. Or 'white flags' as they're better known.

Graham Cann

GROWING OLD

I'm so old that when I go to a café to order a three minute boiled egg, they want the money up front.

First you forget names, then you forget faces. Next you forget to pull up your flies and finally you forget to pull them down.

I was always taught to respect my elders but I've reached the age when I don't have anyone to respect.

I'm a three-times-a-night man. That toilet light is hardly ever off.

I was at an ATM machine yesterday when a little old lady asked if I could check her balance so I pushed her over.

When I was a boy, the Dead Sea was only sick.

The only reason I've taken up jogging is so I can hear heavy breathing again.

You know you're getting old when the candles cost more than the cake.

I don't plan to grow old gracefully. I plan to have face lifts until my ears meet.

An archaeologist is the best husband a woman can have. The older she gets, the more interesting he is in her.

At my age, flowers scare me.

HAPPINESS

I'd give my right arm to be ambidextrous.

Arriving at work today a clown opened the door for me. I thought 'That's a nice jester'.

Statistically, 6 out of 7 dwarfs are not happy.

Happiness is sunshine, a good meal and a good or a bad woman. It depends how much happiness you can handle.

Why was the horse so happy? Because he lived in a stable environment.

Some people light up a room when they enter it. Other people do so when they leave.

Ecstasy: Happiness with its clothes off.

HEALTH

If I'm ever feeling down, I just type 'Yo are the best' into Google. It then responds 'I think you mean "you are the best"' and I feel so much better.

I've been taking Viagra for my sunburn. It doesn't cure it but during the night it keeps the sheets off my legs.

I've just started up an STD clinic from scratch.

The problem isn't that obesity runs in your family. The problem is no-one runs in your family.

My psychiatrist says I have a preoccupation with vengeance. We'll see about that!

I was going to donate blood today but they always ask way too many personal questions like 'Whose blood is this?' and 'Where did you get it?'

I've got a phobia of over-engineered buildings. It's a complex complex complex.

Business idea: A home surgery kit called Suture Self.

I've used saccharine for years and my doctor told me I had artificial diabetes.

PMS should just be called ovary-acting.

When you get a bladder infection, urine trouble.

Call it a hunch but I'm pretty sure I have an abnormal convex curvature of the spine.

Graham Cann

I had a neck brace fitted years ago and I've never looked back since.

Measles. Now that's a rash thing to say.

A man walked into a urine sample centre yesterday and stole five bottles of urine but then returned the empty bottles. He was just taking the piss.

I know a man who's got jelly in one ear and custard in the other. He's a trifle deaf.

I ate a couple of Scotch eggs earlier. The nurse in the Glasgow fertility clinic looked sickened.

Never under any circumstances take a sleeping pill and a laxative on the same night.

PMS jokes aren't funny. Period.

The man who invented throat lozenges died last week. There was no coffin at the funeral.

Good health is merely the slowest possible rate at which you can die.

I used to be schizophrenic but we're alright now.

I rushed to hospital today to see my uncle who'd been run over by a steamroller. 'Yes' explained the nurse. 'He's in Room 21……….22 and 23'.

I rang up the amputee helpline but I got cut off.

Little Red Riding Hood has been found in a critical condition. Paramedics have stabilised her condition but she's not out of the woods yet.

My psychiatrist told me I was crazy. I said I wanted a second opinion. He said 'OK, you're ugly too'.

Graham Cann

If 4 out of 5 people suffer from diarrhoea, does that mean 1 out of 5 people enjoy it.

The difference between an oral thermometer and a rectal thermometer is in the taste.

I'm totally deaf. I never thought I'd hear myself say that.

Conjunctivitis.com. That's a site for sore eyes.

I keep randomly shouting out 'broccoli' and 'cauliflower'. I think I might have florets.

What's red and bad for your teeth? A brick.

I recently made a tasteless joke at an alopecia conference. Fortunately it didn't raise any eyebrows.

I've just been prescribed anti-gloating cream. I can't wait to rub it in.

I've just finished a ten week course with my speech therapist and I can't say thank you enough.

The worst time to have a heart attack is playing charades.

Graham Cann

HISTORY

Cleopatra used to bathe in goats' milk. She once fell asleep in the Jacuzzi and woke up in a tub of butter.

I'm learning to joust in the evenings. Well, it's actually knight classes.

The animated history of The Hundred Years War – a long drawn out battle.

I Googled 'Missing Medieval Servant' and it came up with 'Page Not Found'.

Jousting. That's what Brummies ask bees.

Why did Karl Marx dislike Earl Grey tea? Because proper tea is theft.

HOBBIES

I have a step ladder. Obviously, it's not my *real* ladder.

I love games. Last week I ate a chess set but it was horrible so I took it back to the shop. I said 'It's stale mate'. He said 'Are you sure?' I said 'Check mate'.

If you don't know what Morris Dancing is, imagine eight guys from the Ku Klux Klan got lost, ended up at gay pride and just tried to style it out.

My favourite exercise is a combination of a lunge and a crunch. It's called lunch.

I was playing chess with my friend and he said 'Let's make this interesting'. So we stopped playing chess.

Graham Cann

I was watching the London Marathon and saw one runner dressed as a chicken and another runner dressed as an egg. I thought 'This could be interesting'.

If I have one vice, it's to be screwed against the side of a workbench.

I put a dart board on my ceiling yesterday but I don't like using it. It makes me throw up.

I'm really into grandfather clocks – big time.

I'm glad I know sign language. It could come in handy.

If you haven't worn a blindfold at a shooting range before, you should do it. You don't know what you're missing.

My dad's hobby was collecting empty bottles which sounds better than 'alcoholic'.

Standing in a park, I was wondering why a Frisbee gets larger the closer it gets. And then it hit me.

Bonsai lovers are very tolerant people. They hate bigotry.

If I ever see a jogger smiling, I'll consider it.

What's most dangerous about swimming pools? Depends……

What goes around, comes around. Look at Swingball.

Last night I played poker with tarot cards. I got a full house and four people died.

Graham Cann

Recently I went fell walking in the Lake District. That's not strictly true. I actually fell, walking in the Lake District.

HOLIDAYS

I wanted to sue the airline because they damaged my luggage. When I showed the badly damaged remains to my lawyer he said 'You don't really have much of a case'.

I've just been on a cycling holiday. It was the most exhausting thing I have ever done in my entire life. I've got to get a smaller caravan.

I went to the local hotel and said 'Can you put me up?' He then nailed me to the ceiling.

I went to the airport information desk. I said 'How many airports are there in the world?'

How do you get off a non-stop flight?

Graham Cann

I'll tell you what I love doing more than anything – trying to pack myself into a small suitcase. I can hardly contain myself.

I thought Tom Cruise was a boating holiday for male cats.

I went on a holiday with my horse. It was self-cantering.

You know when you go to the seaside, there are two flags stuck in the sand and there's a sign nearby that says you can swim between the flags. I don't take any notice of them. I swim in the sea.

I've just been on a once-in-a-lifetime holiday. Never again!

Last year I went on a ballooning holiday. I put on four stone.

Recently I went on a barging holiday. I haven't got a boat. I just kept barging into people.

HUMAN BODY

If you ever get cold, stand in the corner of a room for a while. They're normally around 90 degrees.

The shinbone is a device for finding furniture in a dark room.

The two red corpuscles. They love in vein.

When I was younger, I felt like a man trapped in a woman's body. Then I was born.

Something guaranteed to warm your heart – electrically heated lungs.

On the other hand, you have different fingers.

Graham Cann

I used to think my brain was the most important organ in my body. Then I thought 'Look who's telling me that!'

I don't like my hands. I always keep them at arm's length.

There's only one use for hippies. To hang your leggies on.

I recently bought a wig made entirely from bum hairs but it keeps blowing off.

Why is it that your nose runs but your feet smell?

I was thinking about getting a brain transplant and then I changed my mind.

I said to the gym instructor 'Can you teach me to do the splits?' He said 'How flexible are you?' I said 'I can make Tuesdays'.

JOBS

A fireman runs into a classroom holding a screwdriver and yelling 'Quick, everyone get out! This is not a drill!'

There was this constipated accountant who tried to work it out with a pencil but he couldn't budget.

I used to sell loose onions till I got the sack.

I decided to leave my job at the helium factory. I refused to be spoken to in that tone of voice.

An archaeologist. Someone whose career lies in ruins.

First thing today, there was a tap on my door. My plumber's got a weird sense of humour.

Graham Cann

What must you know to be a good auctioneer? Lots.

I got an odd-job man in. He was useless. I gave him a list of 8 things to do and he only did numbers 1, 3, 5 and 7.

I've decided to quit my job as a personal trainer because I wasn't big enough or strong enough. I've just handed in my too weak notice.

I've got a new job with 500 people under me. I cut the grass at the cemetery.

A librarian slipped and fell on the library floor. She was in the non-friction section.

How do astronomers organise a party? They planet.

I've got a new job helping out a one-armed typist whenever she wants to do capital letters. It's shift work.

This bloke said to me he was going to be a chimney sweep. I said 'Soot yourself'.

My dad said 'Always leave them wanting more'. Ironically that's how he lost his job in disaster relief.

The soldier who survived mustard gas and pepper spray is now a seasoned veteran.

My first job was in an orange juice factory. They fired me because I couldn't concentrate.

I can't believe I got fired from the calendar factory. All I did was take a day off.

I was in the army once and the sergeant said to me 'What does surrender mean?' I said 'I give up'.

I always knew I'd never become a lawyer. I struggle to pass a bar.

Graham Cann

I've been working for an Arab dairy farmer or Milk Sheikh as he prefers to be called.

My mate's a safety officer in a kids' playground. His career's on the slide.

People think I'm a motorbike stuntman 'always pulling wheelies'. I tell them I'm really just a bin man.

It's 'Jamaican Hairstyle Day' at work tomorrow. I'm dreading it.

I couldn't believe my dad had been stealing from his job as a road worker but when I got home, all the signs were there.

My mate went a bit off the rails when he was younger which is probably why he's no longer a train driver.

I was always taking notes at my last job but then they checked the till……………….

I used to be a freelance journalist but I wasn't very successful. Lance is still in prison.

My friend tries hard to get to work early to beat the crowds. He's loving his new job with the riot police.

I start a new job in Seoul next week. I thought it was a good Korea move.

My friend opened up an ice rink charging just 10p a go. What a cheap skate!

I tried starting up a chicken dating agency but it failed. It was a struggle to make hens meet.

I've got a new job crushing soft fizzy drink cans. It soda pressing.

Graham Cann

The water's so hard where we live, the plumbers have to go round in pairs.

I used to be a banker but over time I lost interest.

I had to quit my job at the shoe recycling factory. It was just sole destroying.

My dad used to say 'always fight fire with fire' which is probably why he got thrown out of the fire brigade.

I used to be a deep sea diver but I couldn't stand the pressure.

I refuse to work down a coal mine. It's beneath me.

Inspecting mirrors is a job I can see myself doing.

A train stops at a train station. A bus stops at a bus station. Now why is my desk called a 'work station'?

I'm going to join the Navy purely out of spite. I'm going to become a Petty Officer.

I used to be a motorcycle courier. Boy, those things are heavy!

<u>LAW AND ORDER</u>

My local police chief has just finished a talk on heroin. I couldn't understand any of it.

What's the difference between unlawful and illegal? Unlawful is against the law. Illegal is a sick bird.

Someone stole my mood ring. I don't know how I feel about that.

A prisoner with a stutter died in prison......before he could finish his sentence.

Two tons of human hair destined for a wig maker has been stolen. Police are combing the area.

Police have just arrested the world tongue-twister champion. I imagine he'll be given a tough sentence   .

It's good news for the man who was jailed for five years for stealing records. He's being re-released next Tuesday.

A man has been found beaten to death in a tent at the V Festival. Is that murder or assault within tent?

Thieves broke in to the luxury home of a budgerigar cage millionaire. He said they totally cleaned him out.

This policeman came up to me with a pencil and a very thin piece of paper. He said 'I want you to trace someone for me'.

Recently in court I was found guilty of being egotistical. I am appealing.

Crime in multi storey car parks. That's wrong on so many levels.

A Muslim and a small rodent with an eyepatch are being hunted by police after a robbery. Police have advised people not to approach them as they are Ahmed and Dangermouse.

After assessing the gas explosion in Salford, police have estimated it caused at least half a million pounds worth of improvements.

To the guy on crutches dressed in camouflage who stole my bag. You can hide but you can't run.

A police officer pulled me over and knocked on my window. I said 'One minute, I'm on the phone'.

Terry Trickster pleaded not guilty to turning the clock back on a number of cars at his garage in Chelsea. He stated that at the time of the offence he was 10,000 miles away in Fulham.

An attempted break-in at the wages office of a timber yard was foiled today by a workman with a chainsaw. Police are looking for a sawn-off man with a shotgun.

A Chinese man has just been found murdered in a storage cupboard. He was taken by supplies.

A man was arrested for stealing helium balloons. Police held him for a while and then let him go.

Did you hear about the mad Mexican train murderer? He had locomotives.

Police are hunting a Knitting Needle Nutter who stabbed six people in the arse recently. They believe the attacker could be following some kind of pattern.

The only way prisoners can call each other is on cell phones.

Police can reveal that five armed men have been arrested near the Sellafield nuclear site in Cumbria. Crickey, I thought the three-eyed fish theory was a joke.

A dog walker was found dead in the local park. Police found the dog but, as yet, they have no lead.

Is someone who steals dogs, cats and other domestic animals a petty criminal?

The tiles A, E, I, O, and U were discovered today in a dead Scrabble player's stomach. Vowel play is suspected.

A suspect was charged today with killing a man with sandpaper. In his defence he said 'I only meant to rough him up a bit'.

A man was in court this morning for stealing a bag. It took just three minutes to get sentenced. It was a briefcase.

Police arrested two kids yesterday – one for drinking battery acid, the other was eating fireworks. They charged one and let the other one off.

Some people say I've got the legs of a dancer. But until they find the rest of the body, the police have got nothing on me.

When you go to court, you're putting yourself in the hands of 12 people who weren't smart enough to get out of jury service.

I was once caught stealing a horse. It was a fair clop.

A man just assaulted me with milk, cream and butter. How dairy?

Graham Cann

MEN

The problem is that God gave men a brain and a penis and only enough blood to run one at a time.

Never hit a man with glasses. Hit him with a baseball bat.

Anniversaries and toilets have one thing in common. Men always miss them.

Why are gays so well dressed? They didn't spend all that time in the closet for nothing.

I just asked my husband if he remembers what day it is today. Scaring men is easy!

Whenever I see a man with a beard, moustache and glasses I think 'There's a man who's taken every precaution to avoid people doodling on photographs of him'.

I'm not a very muscular man. The strongest thing about me is my password.

The way to a man's heart is through his hanky pocket with a bread knife.

The man who had fallen into an upholstery machine is now said to be fully recovered.

A man was found lying in a Soho gutter last night wearing a latex wetsuit, wellingtons and a rubber gas mask. He was found not guilty of being drunk but was fined £100 for having less than the required depth of tread.

A Scottish paedophile has raised a dispute with eBay. The Wii GameBoy he received wasn't quite what he was hoping for.

To the man who invented zero. Thanks for nothing.

A man knocked at my door and asked for a small donation for the local swimming pool. So I gave him a glass of water.

What did the pirate say when he turned 80? Aye matey.

I just met a fat, alcoholic transvestite. He wants to eat, drink and be Mary.

Why are pirates so mean? They just arrrrrr!

Why is a man who invests all your money called a broker?

This man came up to me and asked for a lift. I said 'Sure. You look fantastic, chase your dreams, go for it!'

MIXED BAG

Sincerity is everything. If you can fake that, you've got it made.

I'm not a great fan of sexual innuendoes but occasionally I try and slip one in.

Why was six scared of seven? Because seven ate nine.

What anti-perspirant do pessimists use? Not Sure.

Who says nothing is impossible? I've been doing nothing for years.

Never iron a four leaf clover. You don't want to press your luck.

Graham Cann

I hate Russian dolls. They're so full of themselves.

My colleague can no longer attend next week's Innuendo Seminar so I'm going to have to fill her slot instead.

What's the difference between ignorance and apathy? I don't know and I don't care.

I got shown round an empty perfume factory. It made no scents whatsoever.

I just found out I'm colour blind. It came right out of the green.

I tried to catch some fog. I mist.

A clear conscience is usually the sign of a bad memory.

I rang my local building firm. I said 'I want a skip outside my house'. He said 'I'm not stopping you'.

Yesterday evening I had to change a lightbulb, a bit later I crossed the road, then I walked into a bar. I began to realise my life was one big joke.

My Ultra Sensitive toothpaste doesn't like it when I use other toothpastes.

Plan to be spontaneous..............tomorrow.

A conscience is what hurts when all your other parts feel good.

Parallel lines have so much in common. It's a shame they'll never meet.

There are two rules for success: 1. Don't tell all you know.

What's brown and runs round a field? A fence.

Honesty may be the best policy but it's important to remember that apparently, by elimination, dishonesty is the second best policy.

Who remembers when X Factor was just a Roman sun cream.

My local village was destroyed by toilet paper. Everyone was wiped out.

Life's a bitch. If it was a slut, it'd be easy.

I received a leaflet on anger management the other day. I lost it.

Does the name Pavlov ring a bell?

Nostalgia isn't what it used to be.

I can't remember how to write 1, 1000, 51, 6 and 500 in Roman numerals. I'M LIVID!

What's brown and sounds like a bell? Dung!

I, for one, like Roman numerals.

What's brown and sticky? A stick.

Corduroy pillows are making headlines.

This bouncer said to me 'I'm going to have to ask you to leave'. I said 'Why?' He said 'I have no idea who you are and this is my trampoline'.

RIP boiled water. You'll be mist.

I'm very proud of the English educational system we have today. It's by far the goodest in the world.

I think bad spellers should be allowed to form an onion.

So what if I can't spell Armageddon. It's not the end of the world.

I've just got hold of a lorry load of flat batteries. They were free of charge.

An escalator can never break. It can only become stairs.

Do Transformers get car or life insurance?

A man entered a local paper's pun contest. He sent in 10 different puns in the hope that at least one of the puns would win. Unfortunately, no pun in 10 did.

Two aerials met on a roof, fell in love and got married. The reception was brilliant.

Whatever you're do, always give 100%. Unless you're giving blood.....

Graham Cann

MUSIC

My favourite Russian song is 'Crimea River'.

Adam Ant's new diet book contains this ground breaking advice: 'Don't chew ever, don't chew ever....................'

There's a new Elbow tribute band called Arse. They're so good, you can't tell them apart.

I sold my guitar today to a bloke with no arms. I asked how it was going to work and he said 'I play by ear'.

I've spent all day searching for my U2 CD. But I still haven't found what I'm looking for.

This bloke said to me 'I'm going to attack you with the neck of my guitar'. I said 'Is that a fret?'

When my girlfriend said she was leaving because of my obsession with the Monkees, I thought she was joking. Then I saw her face.......

When you drop a grand piano down a coal mine, all you get is A flat miner.

I've just penned a song about a tortilla. Actually it's more of a wrap.

The worst pub I've ever been to was called The Fiddle. It was a vile inn.

I just saw a large singer with a laptop. It was a Dell.

My computer lets me save up to a dozen videos of music concerts. It has a 12 gig memory.

A driver crashed her 4 x 4 whilst listening to Adele on the radio. She was rolling in the Jeep.

Graham Cann

My mate's bought a scooter and written 'The Who' on the back of all of his jackets. He's having a mod-life crisis.

I don't like country music but I don't mean to denigrate those who do. And for people who like country music, denigrate means 'put down'.

I love to sing and drink scotch. Most people would rather hear me drink scotch.

I woke up last night to find the ghost of Gloria Gaynor standing at the foot of my bed. At first I was afraid, then I was petrified.

I went to see a 'Stiff Little Fingers' tribute band last night. They were called 'Arthritis'.

So I was in this folk club and the bloke next to me started humming. I said 'Can you change your shirt?'

I went to the Royal Albert Hall and it was full of pushchairs. It was the Last Night of the Prams.

NEIGHBOURS

I've just put up an electric fence around my property. My neighbour's dead against it.

I installed a skylight in my apartment. The people who live above me are furious.

The next door neighbour's kid has an imaginary drum kit. You can't beat that!

My next door neighbour worships exhaust pipes. He's a catholic converter.

My neighbour knocked on my door at 230 this morning. Can you believe that? Luckily for him, I was still up playing my bagpipes.

My neighbour's stalking me. She's been Googling my name on her computer. I saw her doing it through my telescope last night.

I threw a biscuit at my neighbour the other day but he ducked. Jammy dodger!

PEOPLE

Never pick a fight with an ugly person. They've got nothing to lose.

I just went to an emotional wedding. Even the cake was in tiers.

I automatically filled the Escort with diesel. She died.

I'll tell you what catches my eye. Short people with umbrellas.

People who use selfie sticks really need to have a good, long look at themselves.

I've just bought the new Prince Charles commemorative teapot. It never reigns but it pours.

1001 One-Liners and Short Jokes

A Rear Admiral fell into a vat of freshly whipped cream this morning. He was later piped aboard his ship.

I've tried telling a few jokes about the unemployed but they don't work.

Claustrophobic people are more productive thinking out of the box.

Support bacteria – they're the only culture some people have.

Throwing acid is wrong.......in some people's eyes.

People say 'I'm taking one day at a time'. You know what? So is everybody. That's how time works.

69% of people find something obscene in every sentence.

Graham Cann

I never forget a face but, in your case, I'm willing to make an exception.

People are making end of the world jokes like there's no tomorrow.

Most people work just hard enough not to get the sack and paid just enough money not to quit.

People say I'm condescending. That means I talk down to people.

Always borrow money from a pessimist. He won't expect it back.

Hospitality. Making your guests feel like they're at home even if you wish they were.

Studies show that 1 in 5 British teens are unable to peel an orange. It's a good job they've all got knives with them.

I ate a ploughman's lunch at the weekend. He didn't look too happy about it.

Stalking is when two people go for a romantic walk together but only one of them knows.

I'm so poor I can't even pay attention.

How can you spot a blind man in a nudist colony? It's not hard.

What do you call a Spaniard who had his car stolen? Carlos.

One good thing about egotists. They don't talk about other people.

Can deaf people tell the difference between a yawn and a scream?

Graham Cann

I've just made a killing selling my shares in the nitrous oxide market. I'll be laughing all the way to the bank.

I recently bought a suicide bed. Each morning I have to talk myself out of it.

Staff gathered in the car park for a fire drill at the sperm bank before the alarm had gone off. It was a premature evacuation.

The unluckiest person in my family is my uncle. Two weeks after he went blind, his guide dog went deaf.

I'm amazed how many people go to Ascot when it's windy. Still, hats off to them.

Light travels faster than sound. That's why some people appear bright until you hear them speak.

A blind man walks into a bar........and a table and then a chair.

I don't mind people telling me they're gay. I just don't want them ramming it down my throat.

Some Geordie told me he was good at flirting so I threw him in a pool but he sank.

Always remember you're unique. Just like everybody else.

Why don't cannibals eat clowns? Because they taste funny.

The thing about dwarfs and midgets is that they have very little in common.

My name's Fin which means it's very hard for me to end emails without sounding pretentious.

Graham Cann

I've deleted all German contacts from my mobile phone. It's now Hans free.

I was up all night wondering what happened to the sun and suddenly it dawned on me.

People call me a hypochondriac. That really hurts.

I noticed my first grey pubic hair today but I didn't freak out. Not like the other people in the lift.

Do homeless people get 'knock, knock' jokes?

I saw this man and woman wrapped in a barcode. I said 'Are you two an item?'

I once met this gangster who pulled up the back of people's pants. It was Wedgie Kray.

I hate people who use big words just to make themselves look perspicacious.

PETS

I was once bitten on the backside by a German Shepherd but he apologised and even introduced me to his dog.

I've trained my dog to bring me a glass of red wine. He's a Bordeaux collie.

What do you call a magic dog? A Labra-cadabra-dor.

I painted a picture of my cat's feet today. You could say it was a paw-trait.

Some dogs are pointers. Mine's a nudger. He's too polite to point.

I got this dog for my wife. I wish I could make a swap like that every day.

A dog owner who entered his pet at Crufts has been sentenced to six months for outraging public decency.

The owners of a dog which swallowed a diamond ring worth £12,000 had to wait three days until it emerged. With a bit of planning it could have been a nice way to propose.

I impulsively bought a cat despite my allergies. I later realised that it was a rash decision.

My friend told me he threw a stick five miles and his dog found it and brought it back. Sounds a bit far-fetched.

The difference between a new husband and a new dog is that after a year, the dog is still excited to see you.

POLITICS

Politicians and nappies have one thing in common. They should be changed regularly and for the same reason.

Maybe Hitler wouldn't have been so grumpy if people hadn't left him hanging for high fives all the time.

I heard recently that the Houses of Parliament are infected with vermin. Well, that's what the rats are saying................

Everyone has the right to be stupid. Politicians just abuse the privilege.

What do you have when a politician is buried up to his neck in sand? Not enough sand.

Tired people vote UKIP.

To succeed in politics it's often necessary to rise above your principles.

99% of politicians give the rest a bad name.

I've decided on election day to take my voting slip for a candlelit meal, champagne and truffles. I'm going to spoil my ballot.

Graham Cann

<u>RELIGION</u>

Jesus is coming. Look busy!

My son's taken up meditation. At least it's better than sitting doing nothing.

I've got a Christian mobile. It's pray-as-you-go.

I started a company selling land mines disguised as prayer mats. Prophets are going through the roof.

Where did Noah keep his bees? In the Ark hives.

This bloke asked me if I was a Jehovah's Witness. I said 'I didn't even see the accident'.

Did Noah include termites on the Ark?

One thing you won't hear a Hindu say. 'You only live once'.

I like Jesus but he loves me so it's awkward.

I'm still an atheist, thank God.

For Lent, I thought I'd give up sexual innuendoes. But it's so hard.

Warning: If you don't pay your exorcist, you'll get repossessed.

Abstinence makes the church grow fondlers.

The Pope has resigned. Like a true Catholic, he pulled out early.

How do you make holy water? Boil the hell out of it.

The first motorbike mentioned in the Bible was Moses's Triumph in Egypt.

'Hot Cross Buns' was actually the name of Jesus's first aerobics DVD.

Atheism must be a non-prophet organisation.

The first ice cream company mentioned in the Bible was Walls of Jericho.

Yesterday I phoned the spiritual leader of Tibet. Today, I received a large goat with a long neck. It turns out I phoned Dial-a-Llama.

Then there was the dyslexic devil worshipper who sold his soul to Santa.

And the Lord said unto John 'Come forth and you will receive eternal life'. But John came fifth and won a toaster.

I've believed in reincarnation ever since I was a young frog.

A hymn has recently been dedicated to a Leeds corset factory. It's 'All is Safely Gathered In'.

What did the Buddhist say to the hot dog vendor? Make me one with everything.

I caught a Muslim friend of mine getting intimate with a sheep. He said it was Islam and he could do what he wanted.

If God is watching us, the least we can do is to be entertaining.

Graham Cann

I asked God for a bike but I know God doesn't work that way. So I stole a bike and asked for forgiveness.

I got home and there was a dead chicken flying around the house. So I rang up the vicar. I said 'Get here quick. I've got a poultrygeist!'

Why do psychics have to ask for your name?

If you believe in telekinesis, raise my hand!

I got sacked last night from the Salvation Army soup kitchen. All I said was 'For God's sake hurry up. Some of us have got a home to go to'.

SCIENCE AND TECHNOLOGY

I've got a Bonnie Tyler satnav but it's useless. It keeps telling me to turn around and every now and then it falls apart.

Don't trust atoms. They make up everything.

The world's first gay computer game has been released. It came out on Friday.

I tried to change my password to '14 days' but my computer said it was two week.

I saw a woman in the High Street today selling novelty size mobile phones. She had the biggest pair of Nokias I've ever seen.

Auto correct has become my worst enema.

OK, we know the speed of light. So what's the speed of dark?

Scientists have started to install knockers on their front doors. It's because they want to win a Nobel prize.

Dyslexic IT technicians wait ages for a USB, then three come along at once.

I wanted to make a joke about sodium but Na!

I'd tell you a chemistry joke but I know I wouldn't get a reaction.

Doug Englebart, the visionary who invented the computer mouse has died aged 88. Shame they couldn't right click and save him.

I purchased a microwave bed recently. 8 hours sleep in 10 minutes!

I got an email saying 'At Google Earth we can read maps backwards!' I thought 'That's just spam'.

I needed a password eight characters long so I picked 'Snow White and the seven Dwarfs'.

The reason why shipbuilders never galvanise ships is because that would make them zinc.

Air resistance is a real drag.

What do you call an acid with attitude? A-meano acid.

I like looking at a chart of all the chemical elements....Periodically.

How do you make a hormone? Don't pay her.

Graham Cann

The difference between a dog and a marine biologist is that one wags its tail and the other tags a whale.

Beware of alphabet grenades. If one goes off, it could spell disaster.

I tried to change my password to 'penis' but they said it was too short.

I'm going to donate my body to science and keep my dad happy. He always wanted me to go to medical school.

SELF ANALYSIS

I used to be a narcissist. But now look at me.

Note to self: Thanks for always being there.

I discovered I scream the same way whether I'm about to be devoured by a great white shark or if a piece of seaweed touches my foot.

I used to be indecisive. Now I'm not so sure.

If you don't know what introspection is, you need to take a long, hard look at yourself.

If I had to describe myself in one word, it would be 'bad at following directions'.

I've always had an inferiority complex. But it's not a very good one.

SEX

Last night I almost had a threesome – just needed two more people.

Life is sexually transmitted.

Sex is not the answer. Sex is the question. 'Yes' is the answer.

My girlfriend tried to make me have sex on the bonnet of her Honda Civic. But if I'm going to have sex, it's going to be on my own Accord.

The couple next door have recently made a sex tape. Obviously they don't know that yet.

I keep asking my girlfriend to sexually please me with her key ring but she keeps fobbing me off.

Graham Cann

My ex-girlfriend would always ask me to text her when I got in. That's how small my penis is.

Sex without love is a meaningless experience but, as far as meaningless experiences go, it's pretty damn good.

All my mother told me about sex was that the man goes on top and the woman on the bottom. For three years my husband and I slept in bunk beds.

A man got on to a train and sat next to a woman reading 'Sex Statistics'. 'Any good?' he asked. 'Fascinating' she said. 'American Indians have the thickest penises and Polish men have the longest'. 'By the way, I'm Jane'. 'Hi' he said 'I'm Tonto Kaminski'.

I'm so embarrassed. I've just had a letter back from Screw Fix. It turns out they're not a dating agency after all.

What's the difference between a golf ball and a G-spot? The amount of time he'll spend looking for it.

I had to complete a survey yesterday about what I thought about sex on the television. I said it was extremely uncomfortable.

I've got Type 1 diabetes. Diabetes is the only disease where I've had to stop halfway through having sex to have a Kit Kat.

If it wasn't for pickpockets I'd have no sex life at all.

A bloke walked into a chemists and asked if they sold Viagra. 'Yes sir' said the pharmacist. The man asked 'Do you think I can get it over the counter?' The pharmacist replied 'If you took five or six pills you might'.

Dwarf porn. Ironically found only on the top shelf.

Sex on the TV can't hurt.......unless you fall off.

Then there was that Spanish flasher. Senor Willie.

A girlfriend of mine said that snowfalls reminded her of sex. You never know how many inches you're going to get or how long it'll last.

My wife told me 'Sex is better on holiday'. That wasn't a very nice postcard to receive.

The big difference between sex for money and sex for free is that sex for money usually costs a lot less.

Why did the leprechaun wear two condoms? To be sure, to be sure.

Viagra is now available in powder form for your tea. It doesn't enhance your sexual performance but it does stop your biscuit going soft.

My ex-girlfriend gets really turned on by my trippy rave music. She's trancesexual.

If you have sex with Santa, does that make you a hohosexual?

I'm glad I'm not bisexual. I couldn't stand being rejected by men as well as women.

Sex is like air. It's not important unless you aren't getting any.

I'm hosting a charity concert for people who struggle to reach orgasm. If you can't come, let me know.

The best contraceptive for old people is nudity.

Men have two emotions – hungry and horny. If you see him without an erection, make him a sandwich.

Sex is what posh people carry their coal round in.

If a blind girl tells you you've got a big penis, she's probably just pulling your leg.

Last night I reached for my liquid Viagra and accidentally swigged from a bottle of Tippex. I woke this morning with a huge correction.

My girlfriend always smokes after sex so we now use lubricant.

SHOPPING

A woman went into a butcher's. 'I want a nice piece of bacon and make it lean'. He said 'Which way, madam?'

I said to this guy 'Is there a B and Q in Henley?' He said 'No, there's an H, E, N, L and Y'.

I walked into a butcher's and asked for an ox tail. The butcher said 'Sure thing. Once upon a time there was this ox.........'

I think the bravest thing I've ever done is misjudge how much shopping I want to buy and still not go back to get a basket.

I couldn't find the Oxo cubes anywhere in our local shop today. They must be out of stock.

Graham Cann

I bought some powdered water today but I don't know what to add to it.

Boycott shampoo! Demand the *real* poo.

The supermarket checkout sign said 'Eight items or less'. So I changed my name to Les.

Ebay is so useless. I tried to look up lighters and all they had were 16542 matches.

I went into this pet shop. I said 'Can I buy a goldfish?' The guy said 'Do you want an aquarium?' I said 'I don't care what star sign it is'.

I said to my butcher 'I'll have a pound of sausages'. He said 'I'm very sorry, sir, we only serve kilos in here'. I said 'OK then, I'll have a pound of kilos'.

I went to the corner shop and bought four corners.

I went down to my local supermarket and I said 'I want to make a complaint. The vinegar's got lumps in it'. He said 'Those are pickled onions'.

I said to my butcher 'I bet you £50 you can't reach the meat off the top shelf'. He said 'No, you're right. The steaks are too high.

I just saw a box of After Eights on eBay. Mint condition.

I went into a sweet shop and said 'Do you do Twix?' He said 'Yes, I'm quite good at juggling'.

I bought some Bermuda shorts and when I took them off, my underpants had disappeared.

Owing to increased energy bills, the '99p Shop' have put up their prices by 1p. No change there then.

I was overcharged for Velcro last week. What a rip off!

Graham Cann

I went to Waterstones and asked the woman for a book about turtles. She said 'Hardback?' I said 'Yes, and little heads'.

I bought some HP sauce the other day. It's costing me 6p a week over the next 2 years.

I went to my local paper shop but it had blown away.

So I went to the chemist's and said 'Give me some rat poison'. He said 'I'm sorry, sir, but we only sell things to unblock your nose'. I said 'I know that, but I've got a rat up my nose'.

I went to buy some camouflage trousers the other day but I couldn't find any.

I've just bought a reversible jacket. I'm excited to see how it turns out.

<u>SPORT</u>

Shopping for Oxo cubes I saw beef, chicken, lamb, vegetable and Crystal Palace. I asked the shop assistant what the Crystal Palace one was and she said 'It's new out. It's the laughing stock'.

A central European trampolining team have just gone bankrupt. They were bouncing Czechs.

Lance Armstrong has denied ever using drugs but he admitted pedalling.

Why was Cinderella thrown off the basketball team? She ran away from the ball.

Sales of beer bottles and tinned goods have fallen in Australia recently. It turns out they haven't got any openers.

Graham Cann

Tiger Woods has got one hell of a temper. I said to him 'Do you like golf buggies?' And he went off on one!

The Tour de France in recent years has resembled Amsterdam with lots of people on drugs riding bikes.

My great grandma died after completing a marathon but hey, at least she had a good run.

It takes a lot of balls to play golf the way I do.

The lifeguard wasn't able to save the hippie. He was too far out, man.

Never date a tennis player. Love means nothing to them.

TRANSPORT

Yesterday I parked my car in a tow-away zone. When I came back, the entire area was missing.

Virgin Trains today opened their first booking office come betting shop. This means you can buy a ticket *and* put a bet on whether you'll arrive on time.

What's worse than raining cats and dogs? Hailing taxis.

I call my car Flattery – it gets me nowhere.

A car designer has crossed a Toyota with Quasimodo and come up with The Hatchback of Notre Dame.

It was only when I bought a motorbike that I found out adrenaline is brown.

157

Graham Cann

I entered a competition putting sails on boats. It was rigged.

What do you call a train loaded with toffee? A chew-chew train.

I was driving down the road when I ran over some hummous. A little further on, I hit some taramasalata. Then I saw a road sign 'Caution – Dips in Road'.

Someone told me that half of all car accidents happen within a mile of your home. So I moved.

A coach containing session musicians has overturned on the motorway. Drivers may expect lengthy jams.

I couldn't work out how to fasten my seat belt for ages. But then one day it just clicked.

Why can't a bike stand on its own? It's two-tyred.

My car mechanic told me 'I couldn't repair your brakes so I made your horn louder'.

So I said to the train driver 'I want to go to Paris'. He said 'Eurostar?' I said 'I can sing a bit but I'm no Robbie Williams'.

When everything's coming your way, you're in the wrong lane.

I asked this bloke how long the next bus was going to be. He said 'About thirty feet'.

A lorry carrying onions has overturned on the M62. Police are urging motorists to find a hard shoulder to cry on.

I just passed a whole field of sheep on the bus today. What they were doing on the bus I don't know.

Graham Cann

While driving, I had an accident with a magician. It wasn't my fault. He came out of nowhere.

Have you heard about the magic tractor? It turned into a field.

Do you know, somebody complimented me on my parking today? They kindly left a little note on my windscreen which said 'Parking Fine'.

Surely every car is a people carrier.

You know what really floats my boat? Buoyancy.

A container ship full of blue paint has collided with a container ship full of red paint. The crew have been marooned.

I got really emotional this morning at the petrol station. I don't know why but I just started filling up.

The most dangerous part of a motorbike is the nut that connects the seat to the handlebars.

WISE SAYINGS

Light travels faster than sound which is why some people appear bright until you hear them speak.

Two Eskimos sitting in a boat were chilly so they lit a fire and it sank proving, once and for all, that you can't have your kayak and heat it.

The early bird gets the worm but the late worm gets to live.

A fine is a tax for doing wrong. A tax is a fine for doing well.

Money can't buy happiness but it sure makes misery easier to live with.

The light at the end of the tunnel could be an oncoming train.

If you try to fail and succeed, which have you done?

If anything is possible, then is it possible for something to be impossible?

Ambition is a lame excuse for not having enough sense to be lazy.

Without a plan, nothing can go wrong.

Make a man a fire and he'll be warm for the night. Set a man on fire and he'll be warm for the rest of his life.

A closed mouth gathers no foot.

Before you criticise people, you should walk a mile in their shoes. That way, when you criticise them, you're a mile away and you've got their shoes.

Graham Cann

Give a man a fish and he'll eat for a day. Teach him how to fish and he'll sit in a boat and drink beer all day.

If practice makes perfect and nobody's perfect, why practice?

Never trust a man with short legs. His brain's too near his bottom.

Knowledge is knowing a tomato is a fruit. Wisdom is not putting it in a fruit salad.

Better to remain silent and be thought a fool than to speak and remove all doubt.

WOMEN

I was surprised when she put her head on my shoulder. I didn't know it came off.

Feminism is not a fad. It's not like Angry Birds. Although it does involve a lot of angry birds. Bad example.

How come Miss Universe is only ever won by people from Earth?

Women shouldn't have children after 35. 35 children is enough!

My mate married a Czech girl who took five hours to Hoover the living room. She was a Slovac.

A horsewoman decided today to cover her horse with lettuce and tomatoes. She wanted to ride side-salad.

Graham Cann

A woman's shoes says a lot about how she feels. If they're behind her ears, she likes you.

Women only call me ugly until they find out how much money I make. Then they call me ugly and poor.

Women will never be equal to men until they can walk down the street with a bald head and a beer gut and still think they're sexy.

It only takes 3.5 inches to please a woman. It doesn't matter if it's Visa or Mastercard.

A woman walked into a bar and asked for a double entendre. So the barman gave her one.

There were a couple of women banging on my bedroom door all last night. Eventually I had to let them out.

She said she was approaching forty and I couldn't help wondering from what direction.

I have never understood why women love cats. Cats are independent, they don't listen, they don't come when you call, they like to stay out all night and when they're home they like to be left alone and sleep. Every quality that women hate in men.

What's the difference between women and terrorists? You can negotiate with terrorists.

Telling a drunk woman to calm down has the same effect as baptising a cat.

A woman said to her friend that her husband had just bought her a bunch of flowers. She said 'I suppose I'll have to spend the entire weekend on my back with my legs in the air'. Her friend said 'Don't you have a vase?'

Graham Cann

A recent study has found that women who carry a little extra weight live longer than the men who mention it.

<u>WORDS</u>

Thanks for explaining the word 'many' to me. It means a lot.

What's another word for Thesaurus?

Whose cruel idea was it for the word 'lisp' to have an 's' in it?

What starts with an E, ends with an E and only has one letter in it? Envelope.

I can't understand why people are so bothered about me knowing what the word 'apocalypse' means. It's not like it's the end of the world.

I've just invented a new word: Plagiarism.

Graham Cann

I'm very good friends with 25 letters of the alphabet. I don't know why.

BNAG – that's BANG out of order!

Why are there five syllables in monosyllabic?

If Plan A doesn't work, the alphabet has 25 more letters. Keep calm!

The past, present and future walked into a bar. It was tense moment.

Why is bra singular and panties plural?

'Stressed' is just 'desserts' spelt backwards.

Four fonts walked into a bar. The barman shouted 'We don't want your type in here!'

WORLD

A man jumped into a river in France in the early hours of this morning. He was said to be in Seine.

The main difference between Dubai and Abu Dhabi is that people in Dubai don't like the Flintstones but people in Abu Dhabi dooooo!

Why do native Red Indians hate snow? Because it's white and settles on their land.

This bloke said to me 'What do you think of semaphore?' I said 'I prefer Malaysia'.

There are no casinos in China because the Chinese hate Tibet.

Graham Cann

I threw an Asian man down a flight of stairs. It was Wong on so many levels.

I've just seen a huge Egyptian woman stick her bare arse out of her car window. It was a two-ton car moon.

How many Germans does it take to screw in a lightbulb? One. They're efficient and not very funny.

I met this feller with a didgeridoo and he was playing Dancing Queen. I thought 'That's aboriginal'.

If every human being in the world stood in single file round the equator, most of them would drown.

My mate Jim Apple gets a lot of grief when people in France ask who he is.

30 million acres of rainforest are being destroyed every year and here I am attempting to recycle a single jar of Marmite.

It has recently been discovered that Wales is sinking into the sea due mainly to all the leeks in the ground.

A bloke said he was going to dress up like a small island off Italy. I said 'Don't be so silly'.

One in five people in the world are Chinese. There are five people in my family so it must be one of them. It's either my mum or dad. Or my elder brother Colin. Or my younger brother Ho-Chi-Chu. It must be Colin.

I can speak Swahelium. It's like Swahili but a bit higher.

I'm proper Anglo-Welsh. My parents burnt down their own cottage.

Graham Cann

I escaped from Iraq the only way I knew how. Iran.

Where are the Andes? At the end of your wristies.

What do you call a boomerang that doesn't come back? A stick.

Mountains aren't funny. They're hill areas.

A plateau is the highest form of flattery.

What's Irish and stays out all night? Patio Furniture

The best thing about living in Switzerland must be the national flag. It's a big plus.

The Scots invented hypnosis, chloroform and hypodermic syringes. Wouldn't it just be easier to talk to a woman?

1001 One-Liners and Short Jokes

I hope very much that you enjoyed this book. I have an EXCLUSIVE OFFER for every reader who would like a new selection of one-liners sent direct to their email address every week completely FREE OF CHARGE, just contact me at the publisher's email address <u>chascannco@gmail.com</u> and I'll be happy to set this up for you.

I would be very grateful if you could leave a review for '1001 One-Liners and Short Jokes' on Amazon. The more positive the reviews, the more people will be encouraged to take a look at this book and, hopefully, brighten up their days too!

WOULD YOU LIKE US TO SEND YOU BRAND NEW KINDLE BOOKS FOR **FREE**?

That is what we do for every member of our Advance Readers Club.

We will send you a new Kindle book absolutely FREE prior to the publication date. All we ask is that you read it and then place an honest review on Amazon.

Just contact us now on chascannco@gmail.com and you will be added to a special list that we email every time a new book is released.

1001 One-Liners and Short Jokes

Also available from the publisher of this book:

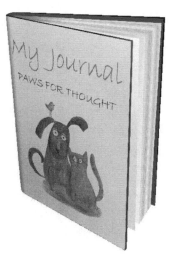

'My Journal ~ Paws For Thought' is designed with **YOU** in mind.

This unique, beautifully illustrated pet notebook has been especially created for you as Pet-Parent to record your new family members' special moments, milestones, achievements and so much more.

All 150 pages include room to record your daily walks, training and grooming schedules with some quotes and jokes thrown in to entertain you. This paperback will be something that you will want to keep and treasure always.

What you will LOVE about 'My Journal':

- 150 pages of quality paper perfect for gel pen, ink or pencils
- Each page is decorated with cute paw print images
- Perfect gift for Christmas and birthdays
- Value for money
- Suitable for dogs and cats
- Ideal size to carry with you in your bag

Graham Cann

- A place for your own reflections of your day
- Perfect for your pet training, grooming, health and well-being records

What you will find inside:
- Your pet's personal detail
- Daily record in detail together
- Record of your favourite walks
- A place for your favourite photos
- Paws for Thoughts - your own pages
- Your pet health &well-being record
- Your pet grooming record
- Your pet training plan
- your pet calendar

USA: https://www.amazon.com/My-Journal-Thought-Jules-Cann/dp/1838090576

UK: https://www.amazon.co.uk/My-Journal-Thought-Jules-Cann/dp/1838090576

AUSTRALIA: https://www.amazon.com.au/My-Journal-Thought-Jules-Cann/dp/1838090576

Do you want the healthy body that you've always desired?

In this deliciously simple, easy to read guide, you'll discover how a Ketogenic (or Keto) Diet turns your body into a fat burning machine and how you can maintain your new, lean look with confidence. The good news for many is that abdominal fat is the first to go with a Keto diet! This compact, informative book will show you how you can really transform your physical and mental health so that you're looking good and feeling good in no time at all.

The Keto Diet Cookbook is ideal for the beginner or for the more seasoned Keto follower.

- **Find out how a Keto Diet actually works**
- **How you can benefit from a Keto lifestyle**

- **Enjoy mouth-watering recipes for breakfast, lunch, dinner and dessert**
- **Discover the foods you can enjoy and the foods that are off-limits**
- **Easy tips and strategies for not quitting**
- **US and metric measurements**
- **Clear nutritional values for every recipe**
- **And much more......................**

Check out what Amazon customers are saying about this book:

"Perfect for a beginner or more advanced cook" ★★★★★

"This recipe book has given me the impetus to regain good habits. Thank you" ★★★★★

"This little book is full of great ideas with delicious recipes. Good variety. Well written and easy to use" ★★★★★

USA: https://www.amazon.com/Keto-Diet-Cookbook-Well-Being-Confidence-ebook/dp/B087XD26SW

UK: https://www.amazon.co.uk/Keto-Diet-Cookbook-Well-Being-Confidence-ebook/dp/B087XD26SW

AUSTRALIA: https://www.amazon.com.au/Keto-Diet-Cookbook-Well-Being-Confidence-ebook/dp/B087XD26SW

"The New Puppy Handbook is the only book you'll ever need for raising a healthy and well-behaved puppy"

When you've made the decision to introduce a puppy into your home, you may be naturally apprehensive, particularly if you are becoming pet parents for the first time. Many let doubts and indecision stand in the way of what is such a challenging but rewarding experience. This is due mainly to potential pet owners not having the correct information in the first place.

As with anything in life, it's easier when you know how!

Graham Cann

This detailed, comprehensive step-by-step guide to choosing, owning and caring for your puppy will be all that you need. By following and putting into practice what you read in this book, your puppy will become a happy and well-adjusted adult canine and you will become the most confident pet owner you can possibly be.

INSIDE:

Choosing a Suitable Breed

Finding Reputable Puppy Breeders

Budgeting for your Puppy

Shopping for Supplies and Equipment

Puppy Proofing your Home and Garden

Training

And so much more…………..

USA:

https://www.amazon.com/New-Puppy-Handbook-Step-Step-ebook/dp/B08LSTMP2J

UK:

https://www.amazon.co.uk/New-Puppy-Handbook-Step-Step-ebook/dp/B08LSTMP2J

Australia:

https://www.amazon.com.au/New-Puppy-Handbook-Step-Step-ebook/dp/B08LSTMP2J

Made in the USA
Middletown, DE
09 December 2020

26961534R00108